TRUNK TALES

Contents

Dee Reid

Story illustrated by Charlie Fowkes

Heinemann

Before Reading

In this story

 Mr Cross

 The children

 Nellie the elephant

Tricky words

- squirted
- water
- children

Introduce these tricky words and help the reader when they come across them later!

Story starter

Mr Cross was a teacher. One day, he took the children to the zoo. They went to see Nellie the elephant. When Mr Cross turned his back ... WHOOOOSH – he was squirted with water!

Naughty Nellie

"Who squirted water at me?"
said Mr Cross.

Mr Cross looked at Nellie.

"Did you squirt water at me?" he said.

"No," said Nellie.

Is Nellie telling
the truth?

"Oh yes you did," said Mr Cross.

"You squirted water all over me."

"Not me," said Nellie.

6

Mr Cross said to the children,
"Did Nellie squirt water
at me?"

"No," said the children. "Nellie is good. She did not squirt water at you."

Nellie had a drink
of water ... and

WHOOOOSH!

She squirted water
all over the children.

Why have the children changed their minds?

"Oh no!!!" said the children. "Nellie is not good!"

"Ha, ha, ha!" said Mr Cross.

Quiz

Text Detective

- What did Nellie do to the children?
- Do you think Nellie is a good elephant?

Word Detective

- **Phonic Focus:** Initial letter sounds
  Page 7: Find a word that begins with 'ch'.
- Page 4: Find the word 'at' twice.
- Page 8: Find a word that rhymes with 'wood'.

Super Speller

Read these words:

did   not   the

Now try to spell them!

HA! HA! HA!

Q What do you get when an elephant squirts water over you?

 A A jumbo jet.

13

Find out about

- How elephants use their trunks

Tricky words

- elephant
- bigger
- trunk
- metres
- smell
- throw
- bull

Introduce these tricky words and help the reader when they come across them later!

Text starter

Elephants are the biggest animals to walk on Earth. They can be three metres high (that's as high as a room!). Elephants are the only animals that have a trunk!

Elephants

Elephants are big.

An elephant is
bigger than a mouse.

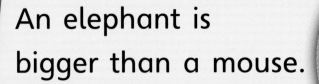

An elephant is
bigger than a man.

An elephant is
bigger than a van.

Trunk

This is an elephant's trunk.
It is two metres long.

An elephant can smell with its trunk.

An elephant can eat with its trunk.

An elephant can drink with its trunk.

An elephant can pick up a pea with its trunk!

An elephant can throw with its trunk.

19

Elephants have big ears.

Elephants have little eyes.

Elephants have big feet.

This is a big bull elephant.

A baby elephant
is called a calf.

This is its baby.

Quiz

Text Detective

- Does an elephant use its trunk to hear?
- Do elephants have little eyes?

Word Detective

- **Phonic Focus:** Initial letter sounds
  Page 19: Find a word that begins with 'th'.
- Page 16: Find the word 'bigger' three times.
- Page 18: Find a word that rhymes with 'man'.

Super Speller

Read these words:

is   can   big

Now try to spell them!

HA! HA! HA!

Q How can you stop an elephant from smelling?

A Tie a knot in its trunk!